HEARING SILENCE

HEARING SILENCE

Edward Williams

Book Guild Publishing

Sussex, England

First published in Great Britain in 2011 by
The Book Guild
Pavilion View
19 New Road
Brighton, BN1 1UF

Typesetting in Bembo by
Keyboard Services, Luton, Bedfordshire

Printed in Great Britain by
CPI Antony Rowe

A catalogue record for this book is available from
The British Library

ISBN 978 1 84624 614 2

Contents

Transparency

Have you ever stood at the gate of eternity?
Exquisite awareness of every detail:
The rusted nail in a lichened stile,
The proud grey grain of a weathered rail,
The fallen golden leaf resting awhile?

The scene, the spoken word, intensely felt;
Awareness so keen no slight detail not seen,
Or heard, or touched, or smelt –
Time has paused when this has been:
A moment of transparency at the gate of eternity.

Childhood Experience

The bare hillside above me soared away;
A pale washed blue allured me up and on;
Primeval urge – impelled to see what lay
Beyond the line where before I hadn't gone
Made me hasty, careless, slipping, sliding,
Smooth-shoed on short dry grass too steep to walk;
Excited, I'd discover what the hill was hiding;
Alone, silence around, panting, I couldn't talk;
My fingers helped me mount the steeper brow;
I hoped the final slope I'd breast:
Another gasp, and slip, and heave, and now
The hill rose gently, softly, to the crest.

Beyond, far distant pastel peaks: ethereal, unreal...
I gazed and gazed in disbelief, and wondering
Descended home, alone ... alone.

Infinity's Edge

A thousand feet below me,
Right between my toes,
Grey Llyn Du'r Arddu
Silently comes and goes,
The clouds flowing free
As the west wind blows.

Left foot on inch of ledge,
Right, in space beyond the edge,
Body leaning on the wall,
Ready, should the leader fall;
Belay, a nylon boot lace
On this stupendous face.

Now mists my world define:
White vapour drifting by
Silently, as the mists of time
Obscure from me why
These two feet of mine
Appear to stand on sky.

Slack rope vanishing above,
Hanging limp to dove-
Grey depths, silent and still;
Dank rock contesting will:
The world is very small
On this tremendous wall.

Note: ddu pronounced (approximately) 'thee'

3

Time lags, seems still,
But changing shades of mist
Measure earth's turning mill,
Confirmed at my wrist;
Yet, when the leader fell,
The mill's timed second
Became a lengthy hell
No measure could have reckoned.

Distance

The frosty hollows
Filled with smoke-blue mist
Made majestic
And ethereal,
Distant and unreal,
Those wooded hills
So near
Before rain.

Evening

Have *you* smelt the wood-smoke burn?
Seen the pastel blue curl and swirl
As the brushwood caught and flames lept,
The billy steaming with fulfilled promise
As tired limbs you happily stretch
And fully relax in evening bliss
As the flames to glowing embers gently turn?

Presences

Listening to primeval presences
Unseen amid the endless wood,
In the dark still forest
In the bitter winter's cold I stood.

Then veils of diaphanous drifting mist
Spread softly, silently dominating as I listened;
But I was not alone in that vast silence;
In awe I turned to where the snow drifts glistened.

Did I see an elusive form,
Featureless, moving soundlessly
As I watched, wondering and amazed,
The trackless undulations stretching endlessly?

Hearing Silence

Solitude of high snowfield
with luminous glow of 'white-out'
leads to uncanny illusions;
so I zip up the tent and listen
in the total, continuous, unbroken stillness –
an eerie unearthly silence
inducing surprising and simple
subjective sound substitutions:
the somnolent tock of a grandfather clock
in a dim and peaceful cottage;
a far away skirl of pipes;
or church bells' faint-heard peal...

The Pass

Sombre, grey, and dark,
A gloomy place of death:
Cenotaph, Sepulchre, Pharaoh's Wall,
Cliffs black, dank and stark
Quelled my very breath
And made me feel so small.

Here the great keen-edged,
Split rock, bossed plate,
Could have cleft my skull
As timid climber unfledged
I moved; it fell too late
And crashed with resonance dull.

Not so the broken body
Smashed in Cwm Glas Mawr,
Dead as the rocks where he lay;
Water trickle, tiny melody,
Silent Cyrn Las, a mighty tower,
Kept safe the secret of his day.

Note: Mawr pronounced 'M-our'

Joyous Steps

Through rustling leaves
Among beech-wood trees;
The spring of the earth
On close-grazed turf;
The crunch of the snow,
The bite in the ice
Of 'front point's' slice;
The long sliding run
Of snow slopes in sun;
The hiss of the leather
With steps through heather;
The happy splash
Of shallows dash:

Of all these and more,
A walk on the shore,
With between-toe ooze
I would certainly choose.

Avalanche

We pitched our tent
Upon the col just
As the dry snow dust
Whirled in our faces
Leaving no traces
Of our route of ascent.

The smack and crack
Of the canvas shelter –
Response to this welter –
Merged in a roar:
I trusted our lore
And zipped up the flap.

Snug in our bags,
After stew from a Primus,
The fury around us
Would certainly not keep
Us from oblivion of sleep,
Though the tent tore to rags.

The deep peace of dream
Into consciousness broke
As I suddenly woke:
Amid the enveloping storm
Had the tent canvas torn?
Distant hiss, almost scream.

Rushing crescendo of noise;
A flash of thought:
'In an avalanche caught,

End in icy grave' –
Time to be brave,
To retain my prosaic poise?

I held my breath,
Movement was pointless –
Just a moment of stress,
My mind on the snow;
What!? – the noise was below:
Postponement of death.

Morning

Have you ever had a peaceful night
In a remote Scottish glen,
Awoke in the early dawn to light
The old Primus stove and then
Crawled out for water from the burn:
Refreshing, ice-cold, clear,
And standing, gazed round, then turned
To see with sudden fear
High flames from tent merrily rising
Mocking the shelter you were prizing?

Peace

Life's sadness and turmoil and strain –
Daily pleasures, the hurts, the duress,
Are lost in the quiet of evening again,
An interlude which is no longer stress:
The beat of the rain on the window pane,
The roar and boom of the wind round the roof
Enhances the peace of the bed where I'm lain;
From mundane reality at last I'm aloof.

Memory Gap

At fourteen thousand feet, with all the world aglow,
The sun shone warm and clear, woolly clouds below;
A ridge invited and on the edge we paused
In awe, our route down sharp steep rocks towards
Alluring gentle green and rolling sunny land;
Over the edge we stepped, cold rocks on either hand,
Left foot gently placed upon an angled boulder:
Then in the cold shade I lay, rock upon my shoulder;
The first firm sunny step; that, I do recall,
But I have a gap in life: a blank about the fall.

Mortality

Infinity's edge, at one with eternity:
Glistening filigree sun-lit far above,
Green ice walls, cathedral-columned,
Pediments silently awaiting slow detachment;
Tremendous power locked softly white
To sweep crevassed cathedral floor.

Twelve times in all I used that aisle
Waiting on a fall, but gazing up awhile,
Aware of mighty forces locked in beauty,
Of numinous nearness, a silent call to duty...
A solitary secret place of symmetry,
Of eternal now: continuity with eternity.

Alpine Matins

That brilliant light on Altels' lethal slope;
So near, so clear, can that be Venus here?
Over the Gemmi the huge full moon gives hope
To two tiny figures plodding without fear
Slowly, steadily, one with the solitude's silent grandeur
Of silver peaks, sepia shadows, and shining ice;
Forging to further fastness of inanimate nature
Their peak, on eggshell blue, now etched to entice.

A wondrous speechless matins to quintessential essence
Of God's so pure and palpably perfect presence.

Weissmies

Years had passed:
Mirroring the passing time,
The moon was well beyond the full;
And Venus, contrasted with before,
But brightly shining still,
Could barely penetrate the morning mist
As two tiny figures' torches,
Bobbing with many an uphill twist,
Mimicked Nature's greater forces.

The wraith-like silent figures slowly wandered,
Climbing the glistening eerie landscape below
To the lighter, stiller stillness –
Of the snow;
And opposite, the ghost of alpenglow;
Higher yet, until a brilliant carpet spread below,
Radiant, vast,
Setting off the intense azure world
Of the sun – about to come.

The Vision to Come

On that Alpine peak we ascended in the dark,
And mist, and silence, to the shining heights;
Now we ascend from gloom and trials
To the blinding splendour of that glorious vision
Not to be looked upon – as we could not there.

Avalanche Birth

Axe thrust in easily,
Stopped with ominous wrist-wrenching scrape;
Boots sank fluffily,
Precarious ice-surface hold, gaiters out of sight;
Jelly feel of sideslip
At next forward step on infinity of sloping white.

Gently I firmly grip,
Carefully rub in my boots and slowly
Undo my longest screw
Then I hold it neat
Between my feet and clip on a crimson sling;
Breath held, then sighs,
As well-aimed blows bury it deep in the ice.

A hiss comes up behind,
Each step-hole joins to the next and the snow
Here and below
Wrinkles like skin
Of aged hand, fragile and thin, it breaks silently,
Crumples and undulates,
Moving and spreading: a leviathan disturbed.

Then as a spent wave
Retreats from the shore, the hollows and crests
Move inexorably,
Innocently, down, break and tumble in terrible turmoil,
Gathering a silent power
Feared and fearful, in seconds unstoppable, irresistible.

Partnership

I gazed on the lichen-covered, moss-hung rock,
Soaked and cold on the mountain slope,
Clasped by the ancient forest stock,
Bark moulded to that solid form in hope
Of support, but seeping in green-oozing moss
One with the rock. I felt ineffable loss.

How long had this partnership withstood
The storms of years, summer's heat,
Winter's blast, and surging flood,
The living tree slowly creeping as deepening peat
And clasping ever more closely and completely
The eternal rock?

Now I stood wet and cold and wondered,
And gazed, at the marriage of these two,
At the ever closer bond, the identity: I pondered
The symbioses of dissimilar pairs, so very few –
Only close inspection could reveal they were not one;
Such ancient fidelity moved me to gaze upon.

The Descent

The inadequate resources,
And depleted forces,
Weakened by isolation
In this cold desolation
Could perhaps be relieved
By a plan just conceived:
One could be spared,
If he were prepared
To descend by The Wall,
Thread the ice fall
Avoiding impasses:
The many great crevasses,
The huge tottering seracs,
And leering yawning cracks,
Besetting his descent.
Would avalanche relent?
Not sweep him away,
Unless late in the day?
Would he persistently try
To find the supply,
His climb be so timed,
That at last he would find
The tent in daylight –
Or be caught in the night?
By following his track
Could he carry them back –
The stores without which
We must leave the last pitch?
Though ascent not a feat,
All must retreat,

The peak unclimbed,
If he wisely declined,
Obeying all precept,
To reject such a concept.

Fear

In the grey light of day
I went on my way:
Incredible solitude
At this altitude;
No sign of vegetation,
No distant habitation,
No speck of light
Anywhere in sight;
In minutes I might be
Upon the boundless sea,
Or, just as soon,
Even on the moon;
Silence pervaded all –
But, *I must not fall.*

Came the dawn:
A windless, silent morn,
The prescient advent
Of boding event;
All was deathly still,
Clamping on the will
Of that moving dot
In that lifeless spot;
No companion's word
In the sounds I heard,
Just the scrape of my axe,
The tinkle from my straps,
The crunch of my footfall –
But, *I must not fall.*

Each side-slope
I traversed with hope
To pass, not retrace
My steps, in that place;
Each surface sag probed,
For I knew it behoved
Me to test each soft
Snow bridge, yet aloft
The avalanche source,
Threat of irresistible force,
Threat always impending
Of wind-slab descending,
Sweeping the seracs tall,
But, *I must not fall.*

As the daylight grew,
Suddenly I knew
This was not just the dawn,
But approach of a storm;
The leaden sky
Not darkness passing by;
The softer snow
More dangerous below;
But what could I do,
Though I full well knew
The dangers of this place?
Only increase my pace;
Overhead spread a threatening pall –
But, *I must not fall.*

The slope decreased,
My pace increased;
More caution was bidden:

The crevasses lay hidden
Beneath the soft névé;
Tread at all heavy
Would likely have landed
Me, broken and stranded,
To freeze to death left,
Wedged in a cleft,
Deep in the ice;
Could caution suffice
Below that terrible wall?
But, *I must not fall.*

Down, down further yet,
The snow almost wet;
I was out before noon,
Not a moment too soon;
Large snowflakes floated
And silently coated
My anorak toggles
As well as my goggles;
I was certainly 'out' –
Six days to the glacier snout –
But no longer there soared,
From which avalanches roared,
On my right that great wall –
But, *I must not fall.*

By queer surface formations,
Over endless undulations,
I ploughed on my way,
Keeping direction where lay
A small tent – only shelter
In this featureless welter

Of snow upon snow;
But the wind didn't blow.
With joy I caught sight
As a mariner at night
Sees a light on the shore:
There right before,
The green of the tent;
Reward heaven-sent!
With joy surprised,
I suddenly realized,
Though so very small,
Here *I COULD FALL*.

Deep in the Birdsong Sea

Deep in the birdsong sea
I am one with the deer:
Silent, fragile, but free,
A doe with no sign of fear,
In graceful beauty looks at me;
Although I stand so near
She leaves her sheltering tree
As I wait, rapt, attentive, here,
Immersed in the birdsong sea.

The Oak

With spreading, twisting, crazy-paving branches' vanity,
Interlocking cumulus canopy
Holly-prickle-protected
Buttressed trunk,

The Oak

When I am sunk
In gloomy thought, affected
By civilization's panoply,
Gives me an anchor symbol of eternal sanity.

The Eternal Now

All our yesterdays
Forever dead
Tomorrows
Yet unborn –
Not yet fed
To trodden ways.

The eternal now
Contact
Of time
With eternity –
So we interact
Knowing not how.

Lovers

What a bower for a lover;
But I scanned the sylvan site in vain
When there strolled from the cover,
Close together following rain,
Manifest lovers each of the other
Innocently looking at me in the lane;
I was so lonely: they stood without fear;
Oh! the content to have seen loving deer.

Brown Bracken

Soft silken brown
Of fine feminine locks;
Flowery powdery brown
Of new-sawn teak;
Polished walnut warmth
Glowing in the firelight;
Horse chestnuts newly fallen
Shining in the autumn sun;
All beckon in glorious brown:
But none can even vie
With the deep burning bronze
Of dead December bracken,
Water-soaked, warmly welcoming,
Intensely enticing infinitude
Stretching to meet the crystal sky.

Green

Spring fast approaches;
Aconites and witch-hazel,
Crocuses and snowdrops,
Herald the spring:
Herald a symphony of green;
Muted opening bars
Of daily greener grass,
Then the darker green
Of shiny shade leaves,
Cuckoo-pint and violet
Unfurling overnight,
Of grey-green buds
Bursting with exuberance,
To convert winter's
Soft and varied browns
To multitudinous shades of green.

Morning Magic

The flush in the east brightens
To bird-recognized new-day promise;
First rays' glancing glints on grass
Encrusted with frost's crisp crowns
Of ephemeral jewels diademic:
The epitome of morning magic.

A myriad diaphanous diamonds
Glinted, flashed, and glowed nearby;
Alone, bereft, I stood, my eye
Then raised to breathless brightness,
Saw the silvery hazy promise
Of future fair in further life.

Bracken Forest

Fine fragile hairy clasps now unfolded,
Flowed to sheltering fronds on sturdy stems;
Crackling brown hillside, summer-moulded,
Invited entry to this short-lived secret forest,
So cool and shady in high noon heat.

No tracks or footsteps sighted:
I crept through margins nearest,
Carefully placing hands and feet
In the deep dim noonday stillness
Of this mysterious miniature forest

And the wonder of that tranquil scene never fades.

Timeless

In the long green grass
I saw the cut-off oak tree bole,
And then could not pass –
My eye had caught the empty hole;
Elliptical, deep,
It broke the flat sawed symmetry
Calling me to peep
Within the depths of mystery;
Eighteen years ago
This hole had cast the selfsame spell
On a child – three or so;
He stooped and looked as well:
What then counts for time?
The hole, the oak tree bole, the same,
Life new to him, great age is mine:
Timelessness, but it has no name.

Waiting

Waiting, waiting, living and partly living;
The remits choose, and choosing, hold;
The minutes become hours;
Hours, days, into aeons;
So beyond time:

Eternity

Already mine:
I retreat to paeans
Of marvellous towers
Above the mundane present: bold
Nimbus unseen except by one most loving.

Signs

Slowly floating leaves signal the year's decline,
Paths' increasing softness, the trees' decreasing moisture needs,
Silent, sombre woodland, approaching nadir of dormancy;
But soon we see the true mark of faithfulness:
New-sprouting hazel seeds and ash's no-longer dormant keys;
Nature's sleep so brief: of growth so many a sign.

Metamorphosis

The grey gritty grub,
Crawling in the pond's green depths,
One day climbs a reed stem
And emerges in bright morning sun;
Drying, it splits to reveal
Breathtaking dragonfly beauty,
A wet, grey, gritty grub no more.

Autumn Bounty

Nature's autumn bounty here on every tree:
Holly berries, elder berries, sleek black sloes,
Wild rose-hips and gleaming shiny crabs, all free
Where the secret, winding woodland path goes,
Ivy-bordered to the open hazel copse;
Where I can reap what few now want: the hops,
Exuberantly shining in the early morning sun
Beside the broken, lichened stile, blackberry-hung,
And yet more bounty beyond: field mushrooms far flung.

Hope

The air was sharp, the frost was crisp,
The sky was dull and here and there a wisp
Floating incense-like, of morning mist;
Reflection of life's sadness, infinitely cold,
Of loneliness, sorrows unspeakable and old,
Of inner ineptitude, disappointments, never told.

Standing straight and clear, a shining green,
Daffodil spikes rose up with brave clear sheen
Of early light, above the drab, cold, mean,
Dull dross of deadness and despair,
Carrying a message clear, of tidings fair,
Of hope: a call to trust in holy care.

The Elms' Renascence

Nimbus-towering above companion hedgerow oak,
As thunder clouds beyond the cumulus
Upheaved in silent grandeur
Lit by lightning flash,
Collapse,

So

The elms

Go;

Hedges' gaps
Where white bare elms clash
With the waving greens of verdure
On the rolling fields and downs above us
Are filled with growth the new elms now cloak.

Cloudscape

Clouds drifting across the background blue;
Serene, silent ships, all sails set;
Purposeless tranquillity merging horizon's grey
Of paler hue:
Junction of earth and sky,
Function of circle's view;
Closer, the crowded day:
Ambitious ability, turmoil and trials,
Cause to forget joy of youthful peace that once we knew.

Roman Ruins

Where the Romans lived I passed
One morning early,
My distant view was theirs:
The Downs stretched vast
Upon the mists floating pearly.

Frost glinted on the golden leaves,
A stillness over all;
No bustle of a Roman dawn,
No cold hands strapping greaves,
No strident morning bugle call.

Where once the legions marched
A silent rabbit stares
From frost-encrusted russet bracken
Dry stems bent and parched:
But the far-flung scene was theirs.

The Gale

Uncertainly I stood
In the nearby grove;
The wind roared above –
And flying twigs drove.

Suddenly, a pistol shot
As a wide crack opened
In the huge trunk at my side;
Silently it gently closed.

I stepped from that shelter
And slowly walked away
Into the stormy welter,
But came again that day.

The giant lay a humble lump of wood
Where earlier beside it I'd stood.

Preparation

Is this all my toil in the hands of God?
To stay and work awhile in sombre gloom,
Yet, of the world aware at height of noon,
The veil so fine, so thin, so small life's rod;

Am I, seed-like, enclosed in prison pod,
In deep darkness slowly growing, hidden,
Maturing, towards the sunshine bidden,
Pod-burst scattering at seed-stalk nod?

To enter bright and open summerland –
Near, and all around, unseen from within
This bounding, circumscribing, curbing skin –
Enclosing growth, its purpose to expand.

To the measure of this great destiny
Guide us, Omnipotent Divinity.

Faith

Your glorious light, the light of life,
A sign unique and wondrous at His hands;
So hold that vision fast through worldly strife:
In His holy caring He faith demands.
Faith! that venture, that step so hard to take;
Did I receive command to do His will
In life's so long-fought fight with all at stake,
I hope, I trust, even now I'd do it still.

But beauty of love, joy, tears and sorrow
Bring us ever nearer that great transition:
That great joyful glory of tomorrow,
When at last we'll know our true position.

Lord, give me vision, leave me not desolate,
Lacking your known guidance, disconsolate.

Science

God decrees, ordains;
Man describes, defines;
With precision obtains
Deeper views of his confines.
Kepler, the planets' courses
With laws precise predicted;
Newton showed controlling forces
Universal, and indicated
With exactitude the ways of God;
His laws stood two hundred years,
And more, 'till Einstein trod
Paths intellectual without fears:
Newton not wrong but incomplete.
Schrödinger, Heisenberg, Hawking, Hoyle,
All strove the mystery to defeat;
In spite of lives of toil,
Mystery of God's way remains;
Man still describes, refines...
Such wondrous designs.

Grief

In loss, in gain, in toil, in strife,
Through joy and sorrow mixed,
We tread a winding path
Of mortal life,
And survive
Above
Grief;
But love
Will arrive,
As keenest knife,
Cutting a straightened swath
Through the thick jungle fixed
Twixt mortal and eternal life.

Release

Faith will assuage the sway,
The dread, fear, unknowing;
Open wide the door, the way
To Life beyond life o'erflowing:
With certainty approach the day
Of high adventure, none exempt;
Glorious! This great episode
No planning to attempt –
The leaving this too heavy load,
Tenant home on short-term lease,
For Life's eternal freehold:
Why call this freeing, this release
– Death?

Sickbed Fantasy

Epitome of Nature's beauty,
Harbinger of those who care,
You have mutely done your duty:
Take the place of honour, there.

Sender's vision vicarious
In misty mind you conjure;
You melt, you fade, precarious
You're gone – glorious wonder.

Aura blue in halo white,
What is this angelic sight?
Faintly flushed, now phantom fair,
'Tis an angel standing there.

Birdsong

I wandered all alone in early morning dew;
winter's snow and stinging frost had gone;
birds sang shrill and sweet, their audience too few,
exuberant and cheerful matins needing none.

Amid this palpable, embracing joy, I pondered
the ever-present love of God as I wandered;
love for each, inexhaustible, though myriads call,
love immense, intangible, outpouring all;
too rarely felt, not by many understood;
even as echoing birdsong filling the wood
could have been enjoyed by hosts, by everyone,
but heard by none...
When at last I'd gone.

Peaceful End

Life's embers burnt low,
Peace reigned in wisdom's glow,
Then amid last wild acclaim
There leaped that joyous flame;
But he now tranquil slept,
And all around him wept.

Visitation

Silent seemed the evening air, clear and calm,
But gradually I became aware –
Through rustlings near and night calls to share,
Above the quiet and friendly nearby farm –
Of some strange ghostly wind's intrusive charm,
Beyond and all about me standing there,
As though a host of angels light and fair
Were passing by to keep us all from harm.

When I had left the darkness of the wood
A myriad helios signalled the sunken sun;
Reaching the hill above I turned and stood:
Aspens fluttered still though day was done.

Did then the aspen trees account for all?
Can I be sure the angels did *not* call?

Sounds

The tinkle and roar
Of tumbling stream or fall;
The rhythmic crash on the shore
Of long slow ocean waves;
The beat of rain on the window pane,
And the secret hiss of fine driven drizzle
From sweeping mountain mist,
Stir the primeval depths
Deep down within.
As by grace my destiny nearing
I live on, trusting, not fearing,
But thankful for the sense of hearing.

The sough of the breeze
In the forest trees;
The summertime rustle of aspen leaves;
The whispers around
As I lie on the ground,
Lie in the unmown hay;
The song of the birds at break of day,
Bring unspeakable depthless peace
And natural unity,
As by grace my destiny nearing
I live on, trusting, not fearing,
But thankful for the sense of hearing.

The soft silence
Of large-flaked falling snow;
The continuous whisper of blizzard dust
Driven along tent's icy crust;

The deafening beat of canvas shelter
Whipped by the screaming wind;
The distant avalanche rumble;
Bring sleepful comfort
After days on eternity's edge,
As by grace my destiny nearing
I live on, trusting, not fearing,
But thankful for the sense of hearing.

The soothing tock
Of the grandfather clock
In a dim and peaceful cottage;
The lap of waves on the shore;
The church bell's call;
The low sad song
Of a woman at work,
Tell me of possible peace
For usually cacophonous man,
As by grace my destiny nearing
I live on, trusting, not fearing,
So thankful for the sense of hearing.

Sight

The silent awesome wonder
Of moonless starlit night,
The velvet sky
With infinity of points of light,
And the reverence, almost fear,
At my insignificance here,
As through a telescope I peer;

Cloudscape vistas;
Mysterious pastel blue
Of distant misty hills;
Symphony of green in wooded groves
And grassy meadows;
Ethereal glistering beauty
Of eternal cloud-surmounted snows;

The fascinating fine texture
Of lichened rock;
And the minute, microscopic beauty
Of hairs and feathers,
Pale beside the smaller symmetry
Of snowflakes and many cells;
But, oh, the mystery of their organelles!

All these give joy in Creator's might –
And make me thankful for the sense of sight.

Odours

I savour the tang of the pine woods,
Am refreshed by the cold keen scent of the sea,
But memories flood to the new-mown hay
And the pungent whiff of ripe cow dung
At the farm at the end of a long long day;
But oh for the joy of a short sharp shower
As I trudge on a dusty way;
As on tapestries of colour, on these I dwell
And find yet more, which I know so well.

I smell the mystery of the long-gone fox,
The tobacco smoke where a stranger's passed,
The raw-skin odour where the nomads camped,
The sharp decay of nearby death,
The musty miasma of fungi crushed
By careless passer-by;
Such are the endless treasures of indrawn breath;
As on tapestries of colour, on these I dwell
And find yet more, which I know so well.

I delight in the subtleties of herbs' hint,
Of sage and thyme and water mint,
Of wood: oak, and cedar, pine; and teak;
And roses after rain;
Honeysuckle on a summer's dying day;
The fragrance from bluebells down the lane;
And stored apples;
As on tapestries of colour, on these I dwell,
And find yet more, which I know so well.

I am so thankful for the sense of smell.

Touch

The warm, soft, fine and yielding pleasure
Of purring puss;
The firm, smooth, shiny black
Of struggling mole;
The tentative, hesitant head and nose
Of timid horse;
The wet, inquisitive, snuffling, nuzzling heads
Of cows;
The palpitating and surprising dryness
Of quiescent toad;
The exquisite folded smoothness
Of frightened feathered friends;
The fleshy naked feel
Of struggling newts;
Even the tickle of tiny creepy-crawlies;
All these and so very many such
Give joy so often and so much
That I'm thankful for the sense of touch.

And the rough-smooth fun of stroking
Newly open leaves
Of conifers and similar trees,
Or the delightful, happy childish skill
Of the one-way stroke
Of new-cut barley sheaves,
And the contrast of the hairy coat
Of unripe foxglove seeds,
The fluffy feel of ripening grass
And the coarse score
Of early, sticky bracken,
Yet more than all, the year-round joy

Of rugged bark of eternal oak
Always there for me to stroke and feel
As gently through the woods I steal;
All these and so very many such
Give joy so often and so much
That I'm thankful for the sense of touch.

The rest of God's creation,
The blest inanimate things,
All allure and teach
The infinity of joy to feel;
The rounded pebbles of the beach,
The rapture of marble sculpture,
And of coarse rough rock,
The sensuousness of driving rain,
Snowflake's silent caress,
The tang of driven-sand-like
Blizzard ice,
Wet mud between the barefoot toes;
The certain grip of incut hold
And the rough-surfaced fold of rock
Reassure as I ascend the beetling crag...
All these and so very many such
Give joy so often and so much
That I'm thankful for the sense of touch.

Taste

Salt on mushrooms;
Broad beans with bacon;
Crisp brown outside meat;
Crunchy nuts;
Bananas and apples:
Tasteful pleasures in plenty:
Such joys so often faced,
I pass on with too great haste,
But am thankful for the sense of taste.

Water from a mountain stream;
Fizzy drinks at home;
Soft herbal tea,
Clear, crisp white wine
On occasions when we dine;
Pleasures without measure;
Such joys so often faced,
I pass on with too great haste,
But am thankful for the sense of taste.

The treasure of taste
Is memory;
Starvation dreams of quiet cottage teas,
Fresh bread, butter, and jam,
And, at the end,
That delight in fat;
Though but once so faced,
Memories many enrich my leisure
And I'm joyful in the sense of taste.

The Magi

We are the Magi from far far away,
We've come through the heat for many a long day;
We were warned by omens and signs up on high;
Our guide is a star moving on in the sky.

We are tired and hungry but soon we'll be there
For the star has now stopped, and the city fair
Must be over those hills and desert sand,
So tomorrow we'll go to that court so grand.

The night was so clear and we rested right well,
But this isn't a town where a king might dwell;
How tiny, how squalid, but look at the star:
It shows ... only a stable our bounty will mar.

And now we are here can this be our all:
In the straw, in a manger, a baby so small?
Oh, it must be the place for it's filled with a light
And presence unearthly, so pure in our sight.

Presentation of Christ in the Temple

Glory to the Father be, glory to the Spirit;
Glory to the heavenly host on high,
Glory be to all on earth: You will it
And the world emits a wondering sigh.

Simeon, the ancient patient priest
Gazed upon, then held aloft, the babe;
His long, long years of waiting ceased;
This mite, all men was here to save.

'O Lord let me now this life depart,
According as Thou long hast promised,
For now this day I've seen His start,
His life for all people to be sacrificed.'

Joseph and Mary in wonder stood
And listened to what old Simeon sang;
The grief to come not understood;
On Calvary's height his words re-rang.

Hymn of Love

Love one another as I have loved you
John 15:12

I was born in a stable grey,
I was born on a pile of hay,
For love of you I was born that day –
Love then wherever you may be;
Love all together secure in me.

I lived all my life in heat and dust,
I lived all my life upholding the just
For love of you I lived because I must –
Love then . . .

I came to my end on top of a hill,
The terror of that day haunts me still,
For love of you I held to my will –
Love then . . .

To a lower state I went for a time,
To visit those of a life of crime,
For love of those who are also mine –
Love then . . .

I came back that Sunday morn,
I came back, I'd weathered the storm,
For love of you I had changed my form –
Love then . . .

I then came on to this higher fate,
To be at the greatest visionary state,
For love of you I still watch your fate –
Love then . . .

A New Prisoner

He moved carefully: I saw him pass
As though treading on broken glass,
Or barefoot in a stubble field;
Silent, others' ills he healed;
Tough and strong, their work he did;
Within long-sleeved smock he hid,
Hard and calloused hands protruding;
He spoke little, tirelessly concluding
Others' work.

Why his turn came so soon we never knew;
Before the pock-marked wall he stood
Hands raised higher than his hood
In compassion to their mock
As they tore off his smock;
Huge rippling torso muscles shone
Before he dropped and was gone,
Scarlet rose gouting in his chest –
Unerring aim of assassin's best:
Others' work.

But ... those bleeding unhealed holes
In his sturdy outstretched wrists,
Each slowly seeping, weeping blood?

The Gate

I stood at the gate in the morning's clear air;
I stood and I stood, but no one was there:
Glorious flowers, the sunshine and dew,
And soft eye-lashed cows stopping to chew.

To darkness I turned, a tunnel of trees,
The hill, and the mud, the wet to my knees,
But a vista I saw: the sun and the glow:
When from life I turn, to death's tunnel go –

I know that the end will be just so.

Bluebells

I sat upon a mossy stump
In a sea of pastel azure,
A shimmering sea,
Submerging every shady hump:

Under shrubs,
Up the hill,
Beneath the trees,
Beside the stream,
Below the hedge,
In the sun,
In the shade,
All smoky
Fragile blue.

Oft and oft in times of solitude
I conjure up that tranquil scene
And know what it must surely mean,
Such vivid memory of brief interlude:

All pervading,
Interpenetrating,
Encompassing,
Illuminating,
Harmonizing,
Tranquillizing
Wispy blue –
Analogue of love
Of God.

Seventy Years On

(In Rural Surrey)

Grass and nettle-grown deeply rutted way
And grazing herd under a silent sky:
Peaceful tranquillity enjoyed by all;
But a garden rose appeared to betray
A hidden past, I looked, and wondered why
There were, nearby, bricks, a broken wall,
And, in the field, turf-encroached, the floor
Of what was once a labourer's cot
And overgrown densely hidden path;
No effort made to tidy or restore
Either house or extensive garden plot:
None to deal with destruction's aftermath?

A steep-sided crater, water within,
Witnessed the cause of this sad ruin.

The Sacrament of Now

Togetherness in the lichened grey
admiring the faerie foaming fall;
birches etched by lightening day;
the spirit of God was over it all.

Ethereal silence, perfect solitude,
eternal togetherness alone with Thee,
distracting sights nor sounds obtrude;
I have the Presence alone with me.

When to afterlife we translate
I trust these moments will become,
Although I know not how,
One blissful simultaneous Now.

The Holy Spirit

What is the Trinity to me?
Three in one, One in three?
God is omniscient, omnipresent,
But in sharp focus to present
Himself here on earth
Or dark plains of dearth,
Or bright and happy, paradise,
He resorts to strange device
And here becomes a man,
There, a form that can
Be comprehended there,
Always with compassion rare.
But this God-in-focus
Ties Him to the locus
We call time, thus to be
Born, grow, suffer, see
Death, the great transition
To that near position
Not on the locus, time,
But nearly so, hence to appear
Anon in places here
Where He had lately been
With us, and so seen
Again by many men
As told and retold then.
Omnipotent, God also immanent,
By presence intangible, permanent;
How so to us below?
Not for us to know
The how and why of this

Intimation of eternal bliss;
Merciful, His presence felt,
When the focus early dwelt,
But to omnipresence time
Exists not, presence sublime
Equally space ignores,
And opens wide the doors
At once, to all, who would
Accept, if they but could,
This all-pervading, universal,
Inexhaustible gift divine;
Equally thine as well as mine:
Could we but truly know it
This is the Holy Spirit.

Self-Realization

Unaware it comes, remains for ever:
the peak experience, that transparent moment,
antithesis of depression's inward searching,
expression of God's divine spark in every man;
committed to life with no escape:
self-realization.

Misapprehension

In melancholy mood I long for open spaces
For the freedom of fresh mountain air,
Lone oneness with the unseen,
Near but not quite there;
I wish to break
The chains
Which tend to make
Life so full of care;
Yet then I know what has been –
That chains have gone and life is fair:
Into another world I go to see its traces.

Ghost

I stamped up the steep in the steel of the dawn;
far, far below, was my lonely mill,
rising in wraiths was mist on the race –
wisps eddying along on the slopes of the lawn.

As I sprang up the turf to the tumuli
the Ring above was quiet and still:
infinite peace so I slowed my pace;
a lark was singing in the blue of the sky.

As defences I breasted, a homespun man,
bending to examine a half buried flint
bright in the dawn at the top of the Ring,
faintly smiled as past him I ran
to gain the height of the opposite crest.
I looked and looked but there wasn't a hint
of a man, only the lark on the wing
dropping down straight to its own open nest.

Shades

He died a slow and lingering death
Without expected fearful complications,
In peaceful quietude with lightest breath –
Never needing skilful applications;
Thankfulness, relief, for all concerned,
Inexorable decline inexorably declared;
We as well as he, death only yearned,
But for all the horrors well prepared.
Days passed when in bed awake I lay
And became aware of something present,
Maybe the sleep aroused mind's interplay,
But a wonderful all-pervading scent
Filled the room and I knew this meant
He had come to thank me as he went.

Colour Fascination

The intricate interplay of colours:
Shot silk tone-movement
Fascinate;
Pale colours turn bright,
Eggshell blue edges,
Mysterious azure depths;
I watched in wonder
This painter's paradise.

Suddenly there were but distant trees,
Houses, cars, mundane things, just these.

My soap bubble had burst.

Loneliness

I walked the hills of Hampstead,
Strolled the streets as evening fell;
Up and down I wandered,
As with welcome warmth and comfort
Rooms began to glow and shine
Across the cold and misty pavements.

Sadly down the darkening slopes,
Deserted, dark, and desolate,
I went;
Down the time-worn steep stone steps
To the cracked and peeling walls –
Of home.

In the glow of metered broken gas fire,
With lentil soup and bread,
I wondered who they were who came
To those rooms aglow and cosy,
Welcomed with a loving smile of care,
And with little children playing there.

Eve of Departure

Food wrapped with loving care,
Taken, packed I know not where;
The snack to have before I go,
Nibbled, toyed with, just for show;
Study connections over again,
It wouldn't do to miss the train;
Packed and checked to go away,
Unpacked, repacked twice today;
I feel quite ill, with heavy heart;
Now, though frankly sick, I depart.

The Once-a-Week Bus

Yes, I remember the bus,
And the early morning fuss
To set out upon the lonely
Windswept hillside lane, only
To wait a half-hour or so
To catch the steaming bus and go
On market day all the way
To town, and, wide-eyed, stay
And gaze on busy traffic stops
Amid the stalls and lighted shops
Until the middle afternoon
(It was often all too soon).

With market baskets on the rack
We all prepared to journey back –
Covers flapping like part-furled sails
Towards the hills where the engine fails,
Which we all enjoy as we push
Since none at all are in a rush.

Now and then the bus broke down:
We had to walk part-way from town,
Also, on the wintry ice,
It had to leave us once or twice;
But through it all we made no fuss –
We dearly loved our ancient bus.

Escalators

Jammed in that upward-moving fraternity
I caught the eye
Of her moving by,
Downward;
Soul met soul then;
An age passed when
We gazed through a hole in eternity.